AF407899

THE THREE KINGS AND THE GREAT GATES OF JUMEIRAH

CRISTINA CABREJAS ARTOLA

AUSTIN MACAULEY PUBLISHERS™

LONDON • CAMBRIDGE • NEW YORK • SHARJAH

Copyright © Cristina Cabrejas Artolad (2020)

ISBN 9789948357391 (Paperback)
ISBN 9789948357384 (E-Book)

Application Number: MC-10-01-9899863
Age Classification: 6-9

The age group that matches the content of the books has been classified according to the age classification system issued by the National Media Council.

First Published (2020)
AUSTIN MACAULEY PUBLISHERS FZE
Sharjah Publishing City
P.O Box [519201]
Sharjah, UAE
www.austinmacauley.ae

+971 655 95 202

Special thanks to my great aunt, Mercedes Artola,
for making my childhood fantasy-world incredibly real.
Thanks to John Spiller and Kathryn Clark for their spontaneous encouragement.
Thanks to EL Correo Del Golfo for supporting and sharing my vision.
Thanks to my dear family, wonderful friends and my little princesses, Paula and Lucia.

Introduction

This story has never been told before, yet our Three Kings have been living in the Arabian Desert for thousands of years. We all wait in anticipation for their arrival in our cities year after year. They travel with their royal entourage from the Arabian Desert to every single city in the world.

The Three Kings, their enchanting pages and their regal camels travel at night, following the stars in the sky. Their long voyage across the globe takes just one night, one single night. It is when we are all asleep, they creep through our windows and leave the presents we have all been wishing for.

How do they know where to go and, most importantly, how do they know what presents we have all been wishing for? Well, we will never know, but we do know a little about their lives in the desert and their planning for the year ahead, entering the Great Gates of Jumeirah.

In the heart of the desert, hidden far away from civilisation, lies the Royal Oasis of the Three Wise Kings who hold all the knowledge and secrets of the universe. Melchior, Gasper and Balthasar are dearly loved in all our homes. No matter where you hide, they will still find you to give you wisdom, the key to our kindness and happiness. We can only see them on one special night, January 5th.

Melchior is the eldest King, the wisest and most affectionate of all. His curly hair and long beard are as white as snow. He is the keeper of gold, one of the three most precious gifts in the world.

Gasper is the youngest and his hair and beard are as ginger as cinnamon. He is the keeper of frankincense trees, the second of the three most precious gifts in the world.

Balthasar is always outside in the sun, making sure that life in the oasis runs in perfect harmony. He keeps myrrh, the last of the three most precious gifts in the world.

Every year, the Kings receive millions of letters from children around the globe, asking them to bring them their favourite toys on the night of January 5th. This night is full of magic as the Three Kings travel all around the world, making children's dreams come true.

The Three Wise Kings work all year round making the children's presents
in their home, the Royal Oasis. It is full of palm trees, colourful gardens,
water fountains and majestic ponds. The water is so pure it is also used
as a mirror. It is an enchanted garden in the middle of the sand dunes in
the Arabian Desert. For thousands of years, people have tried to find the
King's oasis, but no one can ever find it.

The royal pages help the Three Kings make children's toys while enjoying the peaceful and colourful life in the oasis. They live in splendorous tents decorated with carpets and cushions woven with threads of silk and gold.

The lamps smell like beautiful incense and the tables overflow with fruit, flowers and grain.

The pages wear exotic jewels from all around the planet and sing songs all day long.

"Every year, we bring gold to the parents of children in the poorest countries of the world," said King Melchior. "They build homes, hospitals and schools. Marcelino, my royal page, please bring me the list of countries we will visit this year," he said to his assistant.

"I will visit the countries where we need to grow trees and food so the poor children can eat every day," said Balthasar. "Barcelino, my royal page, please bring me the list of countries we need to visit this year."

SCHOOL
HOSPITAL

Marcelino brought the list of countries to King Melchior.
"Good news for Your Highness, this year all children in the world have homes, hospitals, and schools!" said Marcelino.

"Thank you, Marcelino," said the eldest King. "This is very good news. Every year we have more and more happy children in the world, thanks to our hard work."

Barcelino rushed back with the list of countries that needed to grow food for hungry children. "We also have good news, Your Highness Balthasar," he said. "All the children in the world have sufficient food to eat every day!"

Balthasar turned to his royal page. "I am indeed very happy, Barcelino. We have finally eliminated children's hunger from Earth."

Gasper came running towards Melchior's tent. The African King huffed and puffed with all his royal pages following him. What could be the trouble, wondered Melchior and Balthasar. "Gasper is always smiling, we have never seen him so serious," said Melchior.

"Your Majesty Melchior, your Majesty Balthasar, we have come as fast as we could to relay the news," Gasper said, catching his breath.

"Speak, Gasper, speak," said Melchior. "What troubles you and your honourable pages?" "I have just checked the well of love and kindness; I am afraid it is empty!" Gasper exclaimed. "All the royal pages must stop working and start digging another well!"

"That is impossible!" said Melchior. "Our well is always full of love and kindness. What could have gone wrong?"

"Have you checked the camels?" Balthasar asked. "They have probably drunk all the love and kindness in the wells thinking it was water!"

"Actually, you might be right, Balthasar," said Gasper. "When I saw the well, it was dry, I tried to ride my royal camel Groucho, but he couldn't walk straight. So I ran over here to tell you the news."

"All royal pages, please examine the camels immediately!" Melchior shouted.

Marcelino, Barcelino and Gasper gathered up all the pages and went to check the thousands of camels in the Royal Oasis.

They inspected every single camel from top to toe. After weeks of thorough examinations, the pages discovered that the camels had indeed drunk all the love and kindness instead of drinking water. Their legs were wobbly and they couldn't walk straight. But without water, the camels could die of thirst in the fierce heat of the desert.

So, Gasper ordered the pages to turn on the hoses and force the camels to drink as much water as they could, to stop them from dying under the hot desert sun.

"It seems this year we will be busy refilling the well of love and kindness, the key to our wisdom," said Melchior. "We can give the most precious gifts to the world, but without the wisdom of love and kindness, the world will be in darkness."

"Well, we are the Three Wise Men, so let's start filling the well again," Balthasar said. "All pages need to go to the wells; we need all the help we can get," Gasper said. "I will mobilise all units immediately so we can reach the Great Gates of Jumeirah without delay. The crowds have been anxiously waiting for our arrival."

"This year the Royal Parade will enter the Great Gates of Jumeirah with the most elegant camels that the desert has ever known," said Balthasar.

"From now on," said Melchior, "camels will be the most lovable creatures in the desert. Like us, they will bestow the magic of happiness on those who touch them."

"Your Majesty Melchior, do you think the Great Gates of Jumeirah can open wide enough to allow so much beauty inside?" asked Balthasar.

"Your Majesty Balthasar," Melchior replied, "that will indeed be your conquest. I am certain you will make the Great Gates of Jumeirah most beautiful and enchanting, so all the cities in the world can mirror their splendour and prepare for our arrival."

"Thank you, Melchior," said Balthasar, "your wisdom, as the eldest King, is an inspiration to His Majesty Gasper, myself and the entire Royal Oasis. Your words of advice are a sweet melody of good wishes. As the stars have bestowed upon me the wisdom to make wishes come true, I will make the Great Gates of Jumeirah, the most magnificent to allow true radiance inside their walls."

And that is how camels became the most treasured animals in the Orient. The Great Gates of Jumeirah continue to welcome the Three Wise Men every year on the night of January 5th. The Three Wise Kings will then continue their long journey around the world, following the North Star and leaving gifts in each and every home for each and every one of us.

Remember, it is in the Arabian Desert where all secrets are kept.

Why? You may wonder.

During the night, the moon comes out of her sleep and wakes her beautiful daughters, the stars of the universe.

The stars then dress up in bright lights to share their secrets with their cousins, the majestic sand dunes of the desert. The camels listen in silence. They are the chosen animals to carry great kings and wise men throughout the Arabian Desert.